60 FacTs AbOuT

IRELAND

This Little Explore The World book belongs to:

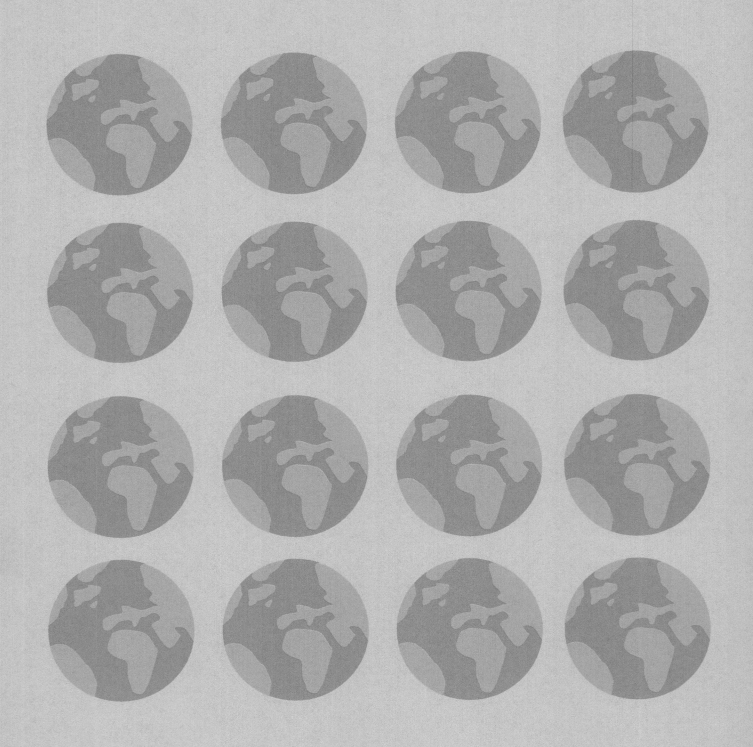

For
Curious Learners

FOLLOW US ON SOCIAL MEDIA

 @grantpublishingltd

Contents

60 FacTs AbOut

IRELAND

60 Facts About Ireland

60 Facts About Ireland

Let's learn something

Grant Publishing

This book contains bite-sized facts and stunning photographs about the wonderful country that is Ireland. A great choice to introduce your child to the world around them.

THE COUNTRY

Ireland is a country in the continent of Europe.

Ireland is located in the north-western part of Europe.

Ireland is also known as the Republic of Ireland.

The Irish name of Ireland, Éire, comes from the old Irish Éiru, the name of a Goddess in Irish mythology.

Ireland contains 26 of the 32 counties of the island of Ireland.

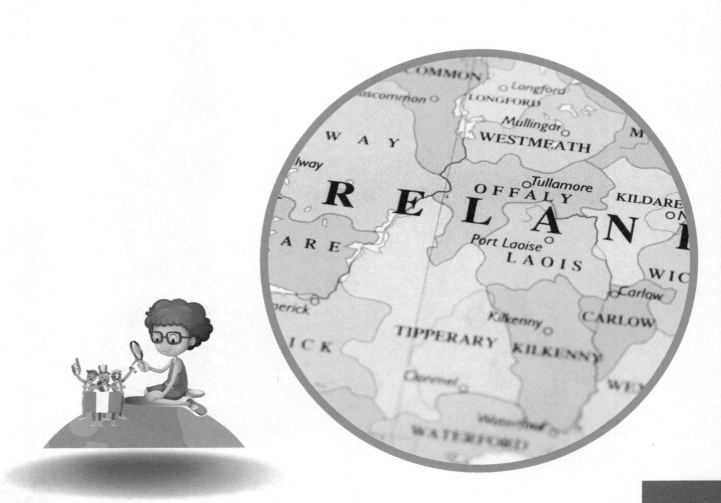

Ireland shares a border with Northern Ireland.

Ireland is surrounded by the Atlantic Ocean, Celtic Sea, Irish Sea and St. George's Channel.

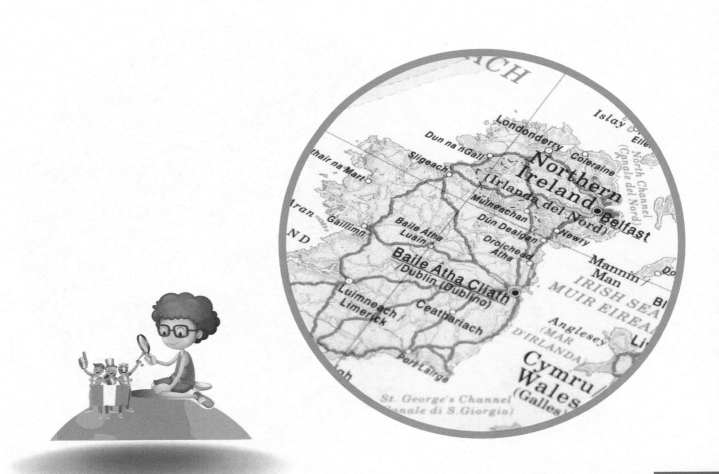

The capital city in the Republic of Ireland is Dublin.

Dublin is also the largest city.

Picture of Cathedral of Dublin

About 40 percent of the country's population live in the Greater Dublin Area.

Major cities in the Republic of Ireland include Galway, Cork, Limerick, Belfast and Kilkenny.

Picture of the Claddagh Galway in Galway

The largest county in Ireland is Cork.

Picture of St. Patrick Quay

Ireland has a population of around 5 million people.

People from Ireland are called Irish.

The official languages of Ireland are Irish and English.

Polish is the most widely spoken language in Ireland after English, with Irish as the third most spoken.

Only 2% of people in Ireland speak Irish daily.

A short phrase in Irish meaning 'Do you speak Irish?'.

The national anthem is 'Amhrán na bhFiann'.

Ireland gained independence from the United Kingdom on 6th December 1921 under the Anglo-Irish Treaty.

Under the Act of Union, the island of
Ireland was part of the United Kingdom from 1st
January 1801 to 6th December 1922.

The currency is the Euro.

In Ireland, people drive on the left side of the road.

The national flag of Ireland is a vertical tricolour of green, white and orange.

The colours of the flag represent the Gaelic tradition (green) and the followers of William of Orange in Ireland (orange), with white representing the aspiration for peace between them.

Ireland is a member of the European Union.

HISTORY

Ireland has a wealth of structures, surviving from the Neolithic period, such as Brú na Bóinne, Poulnabrone dolmen, Castlestrange stone, Turoe stone, and Drombeg stone circle.

Picture of a The Castlestrange stone

During the Great Famine, from 1845 to 1849, Ireland's population of over 8 million fell by 30%

During the years of the Great Famine, around one million Irish died of starvation and/or disease and another 1.5 million emigrated, mostly to the United States.

Ireland remained neutral during World War II.

CULTURE

The largest religion in Ireland is Christianity.

Picture of St Patrick's Church in Dublin

Roman Catholicism is the largest denomination in Ireland.

Ireland has made a significant contribution to world literature in both the English and Irish languages

Portrait of Irish poet Oscar Wilde

Bram Stoker, the writer of Count Dracula, was Irish.

Oscar Wilde was an Irish poet and playwright
who is best remembered for his epigrams
and plays and his novel The Picture of Dorian Gray.

Picture of the Oscar Wilde memorial in Dublin

Ireland's patron saints are Saint Patrick, Saint Bridget and Saint Columba.

Picture of people celebrating Saint Patrick's day

Ireland has won the Eurovision Song Contest seven times.

The submarine was invented in Ireland by John Philip Holland.

Popular celebration, Halloween, was derived from an Irish festival called Samhain.

Irish dance is the national dance of Ireland.

Gaelic football is the most popular sport in Ireland.

Hurling is a traditional Irish sport.

Due to mass emigration, there are more Irish people are living abroad than there are in Ireland.

The Irish diaspora is one of the world's largest and most dispersed.

The national symbol of Ireland is the harp.

CLIMATE

Ireland has an oceanic climate with cool, damp, cloudy and rainy weather all throughout the year.

The coldest months in Ireland are January and February.

In Ireland, temperatures are seldom lower than -5 °C (23 °F) in winter or higher than 26 °C (79 °F) in summer.

Picture of Galway, Ireland

Ireland is sometimes referred to as the Emerald Isle because of its rolling green fields.

About 12 per cent of Ireland is forested.

Ireland has the highest growth rates for forests in Europe.

Carrauntoohil is the highest mountain in Ireland.

Picture of Carrauntoohil

The River Shannon is the longest river in Ireland.

Picture of River Shannon

Ireland has a wide range of insect, bird and mammal species.

The northern lapwing is Ireland's national bird.

The national plant of Ireland is the Shamrock.

CUISINE

68

Irish stew is considered to be the national dish of Ireland.

Irish cuisine is traditionally based on meat and dairy products, supplemented with seafood and vegetables.

Picture of an Irish breakfast meal

Ireland is famous for the full Irish breakfast, which involves a fried or grilled meal generally consisting of bacon, egg, sausage, pudding, and fried tomato.

Popular meals in Ireland include boxty, colcannon, coddle, stew, and bacon and cabbage.

Picture of Colcannon

Popular everyday beverages among the Irish include tea and coffee.